DATE DUE

| | | | |
|---|---|---|---|
| | | | |
| | | | |
| | | | |
| | | | |
| | | | |
| | | | |
| | | | |
| | | | |
| | | | |
| | | | |
| | | | |
| | | | |
| | | | |

**42235**

005.8
SMI

Smith, Jonathan.

White hat hacking

# WHITE HAT HACKING

Cavendish Square

New York

Jonathan Smith

*For Jessica, Alexis, and Madyson. The three best reasons I ever had.*

Published in 2015 by Cavendish Square Publishing, LLC
243 5th Avenue, Suite 136, New York, NY 10016

First Edition

Website: cavendishsq.com

This publication represents the opinions and views of the author based on his or her personal experience, knowledge, and research. The information in this book serves as a general guide only. The author and publisher have used their best efforts in preparing this book and disclaim liability rising directly or indirectly from the use and application of this book.

CPSIA Compliance Information: Batch #WW15CSQ

All websites were available and accurate when this book was sent to press.

Library of Congress Cataloging-in-Publication Data

Smith, Jonathan, 1977-
White hat hacking / Jonathan Smith.
pages cm — (High-tech jobs)
Includes bibliographical references and index.
ISBN 978-1-50260-272-5 (hardcover) ISBN 978-1-50260-110-0 (ebook)
1. Penetration testing (Computer security)—Vocational guidance—Juvenile literature. I. Title.

QA76.9.A25S635 2015
005.8023—dc23

2014026747

Editor: Kristen Susienka
Copy Editor: Cynthia Roby
Art Director: Jeffrey Talbot
Senior Designer: Amy Greenan
Senior Production Manager: Jennifer Ryder-Talbot
Production Editor: David McNamara
Photo Researcher: J8 Media

Printed in the United States of America

# CONTENTS

A doctor reviews test results on a tablet.

# INTRODUCTION TO WHITE HAT HACKING

Storing and using information is an important part of everything we do. Much of this information is important, private, or sensitive. Over the last thirty years, more and more information has been stored on computers. This includes personal information, such as your doctor's notes about an allergy; private information, such as bank account numbers and balances; or protected information, such as the messages on your cell phone. Would you want this information shared with other people? Of course you wouldn't. It's private, and no one should be able to get his or her hands on it.

The more important the information, the more likely it is to be stored electronically. One example would be your visits to a doctor or hospital. These records are required to be stored electronically and to be kept private and secure, according to the **HIPAA laws**. This means that your doctor's office, insurance companies, and hospitals are required to store your personal records electronically, and share this information only when needed. They should also keep this information from people who do not have permission to view it.

Private information needs to be guarded. If the wrong person gets your information, they could use it to harm you, steal from you, or invade your privacy. A **black hat hacker** is someone who would use one of many tools or techniques to gain access to that information. Black hat hacking is a crime. Once a black hat hacker has your information, he or she will use it for illegal purposes.

Have you heard of someone having his or her credit or bank card information stolen? It was probably the work of a black hat hacker. The stolen credit card may have been used to purchase items for which the hacker did not want to pay. The information a black hat hacker steals can also be sold to others. Personal information, such as e-mail addresses, cell phone numbers, or credit card numbers, is often sold in large lists to black market buyers who use it for illegal purposes.

# KEEPING INFORMATION SAFE

One way businesses try to protect information is to use the services of a white hat hacker. A white hat hacker is a person who is paid to use the same tools and techniques as a black hat hacker to test secure systems and identify areas where companies are vulnerable. Any white hat hacker is part of the cybersecurity industry, whose job is keeping computers and those who use them safe. Many companies use white hat hackers on a regular basis. They may even be required to do so if they handle credit cards or other banking information, insurance records, government documents, or special blueprints for the military.

As systems used to store private information grow more complex, it becomes increasingly difficult for the people responsible to guard this information. Meanwhile, tools used to try and hack these systems are becoming more advanced and

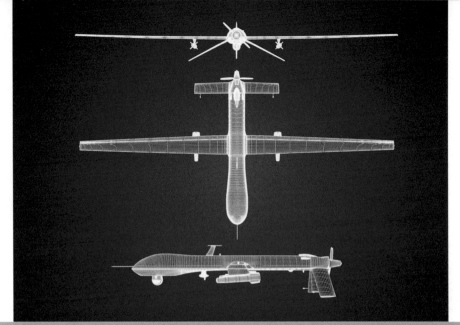

Blueprints for a military drone.

easier to use. As a result, many companies hire others to focus on the security of the information they are storing. Sometimes these companies are required to prove that the security meets a standard, such as the **PCI DSS** standard that sets guidelines for how certain financial information should be stored. Although meeting these standards is often voluntary, not following them could lead to loss of customers or lawsuits. These are actions that could force the company to close. Anyone who trusts a company with his or her private information or money wants that organization to ensure that they are not exposing these records to someone who should not have it.

# LIFE AS A WHITE HAT HACKER

If you have ever tried to hide something private or important from another person so they wouldn't find it, you are doing the job of a white hat hacker! Keeping information stored safely is something we should expect all companies to do as more and

Journals can contain very private information.

more of our information is stored electronically. The rules for keeping this information safe are becoming stricter every day. For these reasons, the need for white hat hackers has increased steadily over the years. Being able to hide personal information from the public is a very special skill to have. A white hat hacker has to possess strong attention to detail and critical thinking skills, and needs to keep up to date with the latest knowledge and tools.

Do you like to visit new places and meet new people? White hat hackers often need to travel for their jobs, sometimes for several weeks at a time. For all of these reasons, it can be very expensive to hire a white hat hacker.

A white hat hacker will learn about many important aspects of a computer system, including:

- **Computer networking** with switches, routers, and firewalls

- **Database systems** such as SQL and Oracle

- **Operating systems** such as Microsoft Windows or Linux

- **Programming languages** such as C++ and HTML (Hypertext Markup Language)

All these pieces work together to allow people to enter, store, and retrieve information. A white hat hacker must understand how the pieces work, how to control what people can do with the information, and most importantly, test and investigate ways a black hat hacker might bypass a company's security. Some white hats, as they are called, learn only a small part of a security system, and learn it very well. This is called specialization.

Many small businesses use network equipment such as this modem to connect to the Internet.

# WHAT ABOUT FUN?!

Hackers of all kinds also attend conferences, or organized gatherings where people discuss and learn about a topic. One very popular conference is called DEF CON. This event is held every year for hackers, whether they are white, black, or gray, to explore new technology and have fun. Illegal activities are not allowed. However, there are often contests and challenges for the black and gray hats to see who can hack something, while the white hats work to see who can keep them out. There are also scavenger hunts.

White hat hacking can be rewarding, challenging, and competitive. If you are interested in technology and like the idea of protecting people's information, keep reading!

Early computer systems, like this one from 1946, were large and cumbersome.

# 1 WHAT IS HACKING AND WHY DO WE NEED WHITE HATS?

 BRIEF HISTORY OF COMPUTERS AND SECURITY

If you are at school, in a library, or even in your own home, it is likely that you have already used some form of technology today. It may have been a cell phone or tablet to check your messages or play your favorite game. It may have been the radio in your parents' car. You may have even used your computer to find this book. However, it wasn't always this way. Before computers and mobile devices were common, even before the Internet, computers were large—big enough to fill a room, or sometimes several rooms. In the 1940s, '50s, and '60s, you had to physically sit in the same place as the computer to access the information stored in it, and only one person could use it at a time.

You are probably used to storing your work on the Internet using services such as Dropbox or Google Docs, both of which rely on **encryption** and passwords to keep information safe. Securing the information in a computer was much easier in the early days—you just didn't let people near it. Companies had well-guarded rooms and safes to keep paper records secure. That was all that was needed to keep information private for a computer as well, because the information on a computer could be stored on punch cards or magnetic analog tape, neither of which are in use today, and placed into a safe.

Fast-forward to America at the end of 1969 when the first computer network, ARPANET, was being developed by what is known today as the Defense Advanced Research Projects Agency (DARPA). ARPANET connected computers at four different colleges together and allowed users to share basic information, files, and e-mail. This could be viewed as the first peer-to-peer network. This grew over time to span 200 locations and is considered the beginning of the Internet we know today. This all changed over time, however. Users no longer have to be at the same computer to access the information stored. They can read, save a copy of, or print out information that is stored on any computer or device nearby or even in another country.

From the beginning, the United States military and the Central Intelligence Agency (CIA) were involved in ARPANET. The first recorded white hat hack was performed in the late 1960s on a computer system manufactured by the Honeywell Corporation. This computer used an operating system, the software that makes the computer run, called Multics. This system tested to confirm whether the computer could be secured in a way that the military could allow people with different security clearances to access it without viewing each other's files. This means that each person would have access to files specific to his or her log-on name. This seems normal today, but on older systems it wasn't the case. During this time, multiple technicians conducted several tests to confirm the system's security. It was found that the system was not secure enough to prevent a determined person from accessing files he or she was blocked from viewing.

Viruses and malware were the first threats to computers.

The computers in ARPANET were the first to suffer from **computer viruses**. Viruses are programs that cause harm to computers and are one of the biggest security threats. The first known virus was called the Creeper System, and did little more than copy itself from computer to computer on ARPANET. It was more of an experiment than anything else. Naturally, the first antivirus program, called the Reaper, was written soon after the attack. Its job was to detect and delete the Creeper. In the next several years, more harmful viruses, designed to copy themselves and cause problems in the computers they infected, were written.

The use of computer networks grew over the next twenty years, expanding to banks, governments, and large corporations. It is no coincidence that **computer fraud**, hacking, and viruses all started to become a common problem during this time. Before the 1980s, computer-related crimes were generally limited to physical damage and sabotage. Viruses were mostly an annoyance or a joke. By the early 1980s, however, computers were in many businesses, schools, and even some homes. That meant that many people had access to a computer, and therefore criminals figured out ways to manipulate the information stored, using it for their benefit. Some stole money. Credit card fraud became increasingly common. On October 12, 1984, the Comprehensive Crime Control Act of 1984 was signed into law by then-president Ronald Reagan. This action gave the Secret Service jurisdiction over credit card crimes. It would be much later, however, that identity theft would become a major problem, primarily because information about people was so much easier to find.

# A HACKER'S PARADISE

Born in 1963, Kevin Mitnick, known as one of the world's first hackers, stole information from various organizations. At one time, he was the "most wanted" hacker in the United States. Throughout his teenage years, Mitnick successfully hacked into the systems of a number of companies, including the National Security Agency (NSA), the Digital Equipment Corporation (DEC), and a McDonald's drive-thru. He had several run-ins with the law during his young adulthood, but he is most remembered for hacking into Sun Microsystems, Nokia, and Motorola, all high-tech companies, in the 1990s. To gain access to the computer systems, he used **social engineering**, and was accused of stealing software worth millions of dollars. With the help of Tsutomu Shimomura, an NSA computer security expert, Mitnick's hacks were discovered and tracked down. In 1995 he pled guilty to computer fraud and served almost five years in prison. Today, Mitnick owns his own computer security company, Mitnick Security, and has abandoned his former criminal streak.

However, Mitnick was not the first hacker. Several hackers before Mitnick attempted to gain access to computers. Although many had success, Kevin Mitnick's hacking story was one of the

Kevin Mitnick was an expert social engineer.

first high-profile cases of computer hacking that involved major corporations and law enforcement. He was certainly not the last, either. A new group of people was emerging: the black and gray hat hackers. Some hacked for fun, some hacked for profit, and others hacked only to cause damage.

## CAN'T EVERYONE JUST BEHAVE?

Throughout the 1980s, hacking and computer crime was becoming very real. Most of the effort to combat hacking was done by regular police methods. Law enforcement and security professionals watched for the signs of hacking by examining phone records and **computer logs**. Most of the time hackers were discovered during a hack or immediately after. All too often the techniques hackers used were not widely known or shared with computer professionals. Although computers were much more

# Origins of the Hacker

The term "hacker" has taken on many meanings, and there is some debate about the history of the word. However, there is a consensus about the way the word is used to describe someone who breaks into a computer or network.

Many think the term "hacker" was coined in the Massachusetts Institute of Technology's (MIT) Model Railroad Club in the late 1950s. Minutes from a club meeting show the term "hacker" referring to someone who modified and experimented with the wiring and electronics of the model railroad layout for learning or experimental purposes. The term "hacker" appeared again at MIT in its student newspaper in 1963, when a group of students modified the wiring of the campus telephone system. From these two instances, people started using "hacker" to refer to someone who caused mischief intentionally. The first use of the term with computer technology was in 1976, in the book *Crime by Computer*.

However, it is commonly believed that the first mainstream media use of the word "hacker" appeared in *Newsweek* on September 5, 1983. The magazine's cover featured seventeen-year-old Neal Patrick. The story inside described Patrick's involvement in a group called the 414s, who were breaking into several government and banking computer systems.

After that time, "hacker" became a popular word and appeared in story after story about computer criminals. Eventually the term started to apply to good guys as well. It is commonly accepted that the phrases "white hats" and "black hats" have their roots in the American movie culture. In popular media such as westerns and spy movies, a cowboy hero would wear a white cowboy hat, showing the audience that he was the good guy, and the bad guy would wear a black hat. Applying this idea to the good and bad guys in computer hacking makes it easier to understand.

common by that time, not many people understood computer security. Many times hackers were able to get into or affect a system simply because the **systems administrator** was sloppy or inexperienced. There was no real presence of white hats then. However, that would soon change.

# NEW IDEAS EMERGE

In November 1988, MIT college graduate student Robert Tappan Morris created and released the Morris Worm, a computer virus that quickly spread through UNIX computer systems throughout the world and effected government and private computers. UNIX systems were very common in large businesses, government agencies, and the telephone service industry. Since they were so common, the virus had many places to spread. This was the first time a computer virus had caused such havoc. In response to the Morris Worm, the agency ARPA (now DARPA) established the Computer Emergency Readiness Team (CERT) program. The first of its kind, CERT was a group of computer security experts who tracked and delivered warnings about major hackings and virus activities. They are still at work today.

To combat the virus threat, a new way of thinking was required. Enter a college student named Dan Farmer. He was about the same age as Kevin Mitnick. While Mitnick was serving his prison term for hacking into DEC's computer system, Farmer developed a tool called the Computer Oracle and Password System (COPS). This was the first widely used tool for testing the security of computers that used the UNIX operating system. Farmer then became the first white hat hacker. Variations of UNIX, called Linux, are used in the Android phones, Mac computers, and many other electronics used today.

In 1989, UNIX computers stored large amounts of data for companies, schools, and the government. The COPS tools were designed to test for common mistakes that people could make, and to reveal signs of hackers and viruses. This included:

- Checking important files to ensure they had not been modified. This process helped confirm that files were not affected by viruses or hackers.

- Comparing the dates of important files with dates of advisories from the CERT Coordination Center. This also helped determine whether a file was infected by a virus or changed by a hacker by confirming if it was changed around the time a hack took place.

- Obtaining file permissions. This helped to ensure only the right people could access certain files.

- Calculating password strength. This tested how easy a password was to guess.

The COPS tool was one of the first of its kind. Soon after, Dan Farmer and programmer Wietse Venema wrote a more advanced set of tools called the Security Administrator Tools for Analyzing Networks (SATAN). This set of tools mimicked many of the common methods hackers would use to break into systems. It might seem obvious that the best way to test security is to mimic an attacker, but this was a very new idea. In 1995, Farmer and Venema published a paper entitled, "Improving the Security of Your Site by Breaking into It." In it, they described this as an "unusual approach to system security." When SATAN was released, many system administrators and law enforcement officials argued that the tools would make it easier for hackers to find vulnerable systems and break into them.

Security professionals could then employ the same hacking techniques as criminals, sometimes without much training or without having a complete understanding of how they work. The line between good and evil became blurry. Temptation to use this power for criminal or personal use overpowered some people. Police agencies and the government were sometimes distrustful of this new ability. To someone outside the security community, it looked as if everyone could be a black hat hacker. However, it was clear that hacking would remain a threat, and people were needed to help combat the problem.

Ethics and responsibility have become a large part of the white hat hacking community. White hat hackers are entrusted to use their knowledge ethically and with care, as they access some of the most private and sensitive information that companies store.

> ## " "
> ## *If you want to learn to solve problems, you must be ready to look anywhere, for anything, and you must be prepared when you find it.*
>
> DAN FARMER

# NOT JUST BUSINESS, SOMETIMES PLEASURE!

Over time, systems have become more complex, more automated, and connected across large distances. In the days of Dan Farmer, many systems were administered by one person or a small group of people. Today, many of these systems are handled by teams of people, oftentimes around the clock. Instead of one, two, or even a handful of servers, companies can have hundreds, if not thousands, in several locations throughout the globe. Instead of a single computer or a small group of computers being able to access the information in those systems, today there are several ways, including smartphones, tablets, laptops, smart boards, smart TVs, and more.

Streaming services, such as Amazon Prime or Netflix, offer a variety of movies or TV shows. Access to these movies and

# Free Spirits

**F**ree spirits are a group of unpaid white hat hackers. The difference between white hats and free spirits is motivation. White hats are hired to provide general security, are restricted by company policies and procedures, and are paid to perform a job. Free spirits, on the other hand, adhere to an unwritten code of ethics that promotes ideas such as free and unrestricted access, less limitation, and creating a better lifestyle by using computers to their greatest potential.

Free spirits hack into systems for any number of reasons, as hacking is a hobby or pastime. They believe that they are helpful, even if they seem to pose a threat. They feel that their role is to promote something positive, and their hacking exploits are about aiding in the overall objective of securing and protecting. Free spirits' ultimate goal is to help identify security weaknesses by hacking into systems and reporting their findings. It is likely that some others would use the same technical savvy maliciously, so free spirits believe they are providing an invaluable service.

other streaming services is protected by individual passwords, and many streaming services can be accessed on different devices. Each service needs to be secured so when you enter your password no one else can gain access. The team of people behind those companies needs to make sure the information those devices access will be safe no matter which one you use. Each is different and uses various security methods. Today's white hat hacker needs a much larger set of tools to test all of the different ways that hackers and viruses can cause trouble.

## "GAME OVER"

Even home devices like the Apple TV can be threatened by hackers.

Equally as vulnerable are some of the more basic electronics in use every day, such as a television. You may not consider a television as a device able to be hacked, but it is. For years, black hats and white hats were in a tug-of-war over DirecTV, which was equipped with one of the first smart cards. These cards controlled what television channels could be accessed. When the service started, the information sent to the DirecTV box was very simply encrypted. People all over the United States discovered ways of getting free satellite TV by hacking the card in the box.

As hackers found ways of breaking in, DirecTV attempted
to enhance the card's security by making it more complex. They
employed white hats to come up with new and creative ways of
defeating the security system, to help the company stay ahead
of the thousands of people trying to bypass security on the card.
Eventually, they found a way to surprise the black hats. DirecTV
approached software engineer Christopher Tarnovsky to lend his
expertise in crafting a creative solution for hacking. Tarnovsky
introduced a "kill" into the hacked cards over a two-month
period—he placed a self-destruct program code into the cards, piece
by piece, so no one noticed what was happening. Then on the "Black
Sunday," a week before the Super Bowl in 2001, DirecTV sent those
cards one final piece of code that caused them to break

down. It was later found that the first eight bytes of memory in the hacked cards were rewritten to read "GAME OVER."

Sometimes the line between white hat hacking and black hat hacking blurs. Tarnovsky was later accused of hacking into the security system of a rival company of DirecTV's parent organization News Corp. He testified that he was hired by the parent company, but denied using pirating software against the company's rivals.

> " "
> *A kill is like firing off a rocket when you are in war.*
> *It's designed to specifically target an illicitly modified device.*
> CHRISTOPHER TARNOVSKY

## SOMETIMES IT'S THAT SIMPLE

Not all white hat testing is high-tech. Even in this age of technology, sometimes information is not stored electronically. White hat hackers will go into businesses to see how secure non-electronic items are inside companies. This often entails returning to the basics of breaking into the building itself. For example, "lock picking" is an age-old hobby of the hacker. This is partly because many times hackers would have to gain access to doors to get to the systems they wanted to hack, or to steal documents and manuals that they needed. Many hackers also saw it as a basic hack and a challenge to themselves. Today, a white hat hacker may be called upon by an organization to see if they can access certain rooms or machines meant to be secure, such as those that store backup tapes or hard copy records. Documents cannot be assumed safe from hackers simply because they are not electronic.

Hackers usually employ a simple method for lock picking called tailgating. This method is used to gain access to areas for which they do not have a key or access card. Dumpster diving is another simple hack, maybe one of the first, that still used today to some degree. Hackers from the very beginning relied on the carelessness of businesses and people to obtain information, and were not above digging through dumpsters and garbage bags to find it. Today, if a white hat is helping to evaluate security at a business, he or she may be asked to verify that hard copies of documents are discarded separate from the regular trash. It is common to search dumpsters, garbage cans, and even the shredded paper file to see if information has been disposed of properly. The garbage is collected in an area, examined, and anything that needs review is put aside. Many people and even businesses still throw away sensitive information without shredding it first.

An example of improper disposal of information would be these findings of a white hat tasked to confirm a small company's discarding of sensitive information. The name of the company is withheld for reasons of privacy. Although the company shreds personal documents, the following were found in its trash:

- A DMV vehicle registration renewal form that listed the office manager's license plate, address, and make and model of the vehicle.

- A few paycheck stubs with names, addresses, as well as hourly rate info thrown out by employees.

- A health care insurance registration form that was discarded by an employee in a break room after miswriting his address.

- A prescription medication bottle with the label removed (good choice!).

It is important to properly dispose of private information, especially in a business setting.

In this case, while the business itself was very careful about protecting sensitive information, its employees were not. A white hat hacker knows that it is often the carelessness or grudge of a single person that can be as risky, or more risky, than any safety measure that the business might miss.

For this reason, white hats will also examine behaviors of the people who have access to information, because having basic security habits are just as important. Look around the room in your computer lab. See how many people have left their computers unlocked as they run to the printer or the bathroom. The same thing happens to businesspeople in airports and offices. A white hat will spend hours, even days, walking around an office, or following employees of a company who are traveling to see if they can get information from them. **Shoulder surfing** is a great example of hacking in plain sight with no technical skills or causing many problems. Simply stand or sit near someone who is using a company laptop or reading sensitive information in a busy airport and read over his or her shoulder.

Hackers can gain information by observing people in public places.

Just as important to the job is knowing a little about psychology. Understanding how people think will help a white hat point out potential problems. For example, in parts of the world such as Asia, it is often considered rude to doubt a person who is a superior in the workplace or who has an official title. A white hat may try to get someone to give them access to a room or information by intimidating them, which is more likely to work in those cultures than it is in the United States.

In the United States, we will often become defensive when a person is trying to get something from us. We may respond better if that person acts as if he or she is in trouble or may lose his or her job if we won't, as a favor, change a password or print a sensitive document. A white hat also knows that if you call someone to get help and they refuse, it's possible that the next person you call just might cooperate. Sooner or later, you will locate someone willing to help.

White Hat Hacking

White hat hackers can have a lot of responsibilities, and may learn a wide variety of skills to perform their jobs, or they may specialize in certain areas of security. They are often the only way a company will confirm its level of security, or what is needed to become more secure. White hats will provide detailed reports and suggest ways to improve security. It is also common for a white hat to test the security of a company that is under a legal investigation, and may not be welcome on its premises. They may even have bad news to share about a security problem they have uncovered, and will need to share that information with people who will not be happy to hear about it. In other cases, they may be working with a company that has already suffered a security attack or an information leak, and will be a hero when they share ways to improve security.

White hat hacking has had a very short history, and has changed a lot over the decades it has been a profession. It has, over time, become an important role for our growing society. Today it is common, in some cases even mandatory, to have a computer security evaluation done in your business, home, or school. White hat hackers are definitely qualified for the job and will most likely be the ones carrying out the evaluation, although they may have a different job title.

The position also has a lot of opportunities. You could be involved in nearly any industry as a white hat. Private businesses, government agencies, the military, and even celebrities will use the services of a white hat hacker to help them maintain their privacy or anonymity. You don't think that Justin Bieber or Adriana Grande use their real names on their personal Facebook accounts, do you?

A question you might be asking now is, "How do I become a white hat hacker?" Read on to find out!

White hats have a wide variety of skills, including a knack for tinkering.

# 2 PREPARING FOR A CAREER IN WHITE HAT HACKING

## DO I HAVE WHAT IT TAKES?

White hat hacking is not a career one simply "steps into." You'll need IT security experience and preferably degrees and certifications. As is true for other IT jobs, employers typically want candidates who have college degrees, but related experience can be valuable. Experience plus certifications can typically take the place of some degree requirements.

If you really want a career in white hat hacking, never engage in black hat hacking. Participating in such illegal activity will "hack" your hacking career. Many of the available jobs are with credit card companies, financial and banking institutions, and government-related organizations. These employers require security clearances and polygraph testing. All companies will perform at least a basic background check.

A good education is also critical to the success of a white hat hacker, and experience will lead them into the future. However, there are some basic skills and interests common to the way any hacker works and thinks.

## INTEREST AND CURIOSITY FOR TECHNOLOGY

While security is the focus, many white hats started down this path out of basic curiosity. Often a white hat asks, "How does this work," or, "How can I make this work differently?" Despite being a white hat, they have probably hacked something they use every day, perhaps a video game console or their cell phone. Hackers of all types like a challenge. They may hack for bragging rights or to possibly be the first to hack a specific device.

## TECHNICAL SKILLS

If you're considering a career as a white hat hacker, you will certainly need to have skills in computers, all possibly even electronics, including :

- Computer hardware
- Computer networking
- Computer programming
- Databases
- Documentation
- Electronics
- Encryption
- Operating systems

Most importantly, it is good to know how all of the different parts of a computer system interact. It is common that a black hat hacker or virus will use a weakness in one system to get to another, and knowing how the pieces to those puzzles connect will be important.

## LOGICAL THINKING AND ANALYTICAL ABILITY

Problem solving is a big part of white hat hacking. Being able to follow a process closely and with strict attention to detail is

Puzzles and other challenges are often very appealing to white hats.

an important quality that a cybersecurity person should have. Investigating a problem will often require critical thinking and being able to quickly identify where something went wrong. Do you enjoy math or logic puzzles, such as Sudoku? Much like a puzzle, evidence of a hacked computer or solution to a weakness in a computer could be as simple as a single digit inside pages of information being out of place. That small detail could be a warning that a black hat hacker is at work. Being able to make sound decisions, having a clear mind, and possessing a strong level of confidence is a must. The ability to solve problems independently is important, as you may be the only person to be able to access specific systems or certain facts regarding a problem.

## SOFT SKILLS

Soft skills, such as flexibility and reliability, are important in any career, and cybersecurity is no exception. Everyone in a technology field has to be a team player. No one person can design everything, solve every problem, or find every fact. Sometimes when you are problem solving, having different perspectives on an issue can be your most valuable tool. Strong verbal and written communication skills are also an asset. You may need to translate technical information to a group unfamiliar with technology. Being organized and planning time well are also important skills for a white hat hacker. You may be required to multitask and thereby need to keep deadlines and priorities in order. Time and accuracy are key if you are responding to a hack that has occurred. You need to report what you learn in order to understand how to respond to the problem. Stopping the hack attempt or fixing the damage it caused may require the assistance of other people and departments. You will need to share information with them in a clear and concise way to ensure everyone knows what has happened and how the issue is to be addressed.

# INTEGRITY

The bond between hacking and security plays a crucial role in keeping information confidential. The amount of responsibility and trust placed on the shoulders of a white hat hacker is immense. It is best not to access or view unauthorized information on systems you are testing, because you will never want to be in a position where you can become a security leak. However, as a white hat hacker you may have access to information that very few people can view, information you are trusted to keep private and confidential.

# GETTING EDUCATED

A formal education in computer science, cybersecurity, networking, programming, or other discipline is essential to becoming a white hat hacker. No matter what area of cybersecurity you enter, as a white hat it is important to understand that hands-on experience combined with book knowledge is the recipe for success. Just like playing a sport, instrument, or acting in a play, knowing the pieces of a puzzle is only part of being successful. Practicing the art is what makes you

Two graduate students at New York University developed this app that controls the fish in the water.

good at it. For this reason, schools such as New York University's Polytechnic School of Engineering offer not only classes in the fundamentals of computer science and computer security, but also host lab sessions that allow students to practice what they are being taught in a controlled environment.

Honesty and integrity are also taken seriously in the cybersecurity field. In the *Huffington Post Tech* article "Inside the Cybersecurity, 'White Hat Hacker' University Network," New York University–Polytechnic professor Nasir Memon stresses how serious the ethical lines are in cybersecurity. When asked if any students had been caught breaking the law, he responds: "We try and create that culture of no messing around. If we find they've done anything, we throw them out of the lab."

These labs are controlled and monitored for suspicious activity. Many times in ethical hacking labs, none of the computers are allowed access to the Internet, and all of the exercises, hacks, and tests are on dummy computer systems that only work in the school. Cybersecurity labs are typically set up this way, too. The precautions are for more than just keeping people honest, though. The tools being used are dangerous and sometimes unforgiving. They can cause interruptions and even damage to computers and other equipment if outside a controlled environment. Everyone make mistakes, and preventing damage to real systems is important.

> **"**  **"**
> *We try and create that culture of no messing around. If we find they've done anything we throw them out of the lab.*
>
> PROFESSOR NASIR MEMON,
> NYU POLYTECHNIC

## HOW FAR DO YOU WANT TO TAKE IT?

The more you know about something, the better chance you have of becoming an expert at it. The more involved and educated you are, the better you become. As a junior varsity football player, for example, it's pretty unlikely you will make the game-winning touchdown in a statewide championship tournament, but as a varsity player, your odds are much better. Much like this, different levels of education can take you to different places in your career as a white hat hacker.

# Ethical Hacking Labs

**O**ne of the best ways to learn how to defend yourself against a hacker is to mimic what they would do. In classes called "labs" you will receive hands-on experience. Some of the activities you will be tasked to perform could include using **exploits**, or software designed to take advantage of a flaw; spying on information from other computers using **sniffers**, which examine information sent between computers to reveal what is being sent; intentionally spreading viruses; and looking for ways to hack into insecure systems with **port scanners**, a tool used to access computers.

Just like writing or singing, practicing your white hat hacking skills means you have the chance to make mistakes, and perfect the skills you are taught. You may even learn new ways to do things that others have not yet tried. The safest way to practice is to have computers and other equipment that are completely separate from both the Internet and computers used day to day in your school.

Hacking labs will have the same tools you employ on the job as a white hat, and sometimes you can use less official tools as well. Many of the exploits and hacks you learn about in a lab can be destructive and ruin the operating system or software on a computer. Because of this, hacking labs are typically set up using **virtual machines**—software-based systems that imitate a computer—so you can reset them to normal operation or delete them when you are done.

There are pre-made setups you can get online to start a hacking lab. One of these is the Open Web Application Security Project (OWASP). It includes tools and computer software that you will need to learn about hacking and testing.

# ASSOCIATE'S DEGREE PROGRAMS

Associate's degree programs in a technology field offered by technical colleges and online schools are stepping-stones into the cybersecurity industry. These programs will prepare you for an entry-level position in cybersecurity. These degrees would require about two years and usually around sixty-five credits to complete, depending on the state. You will receive an education in math, science, and other general education classes. In addition, you will take classes that cover the basics of a wide variety of computer topics. Associate's degree programs tend to be very hands-on. An associate's degree program called Cybersecurity, A.A.S. is offered by Hagerstown Community College in Hagerstown, Maryland. In that program the technical classes include:

- Computer Networking
- Ethics in the Information Age
- Ethical Hacking Fundamentals
- Introduction to Cybersecurity
- Introduction to Penetration Testing
- Introduction to Security Fundamentals
- Microsoft and UNIX/Linux Operating Systems
- Server Management
- Tactical Perimeter Defense

As a beginner in cybersecurity, you may be doing additional work along with being a white hat hacker. With an associate's degree, you will not typically start out focusing solely on white hat tasks. You'll require more experience working with the technologies that control the security of a network. This could include installing and monitoring firewalls—which are security devices designed to protect computers. You will also assist with spam or other e-mail-related security tasks, auditing files specific people have access to, and virus detection and removal on workstations and servers.

You may be able to find a position in a security role by being an assistant to a coworker with more experience. This offers a chance to see someone use higher-level skills, and potentially opens doors to advancement.

Without a higher level of education or experience, it can be difficult to land the more intense white hat jobs, but if your interest is in more than just security, further education is a great way to add other skills to your portfolio. Many people who are in other areas of IT, such as networking, server management, website design, programming, or even helpdesk professionals pursue associate's degrees to improve their understanding of computer security since it is a very important part of any computer job. If you are interested in many different areas of technology, this may be the path for you.

## BACHELOR'S DEGREE

A bachelor's degree will offer a much more concentrated education, both in the general education classes, such as math and science, but also more advanced classes in areas such as computer and security theory. In addition, you gain lots of hands-on experience through in-depth training. Bachelor's degrees typically take longer to complete than associate's degrees—around four years, including 120 credits on average.

There are more job opportunities for someone who holds a bachelor's degree in cybersecurity or other computer-related areas, since these people have a better understanding of the field. Positions that will require a bachelor's degree could include being a network manager, **computer forensics** analyst, senior systems administrator, or network security analyst.

The classes offered in a bachelor's program are typically designed to teach material required to pass many of the industry certifications. (Those are discussed later in this chapter.) With a bachelor's degree, you can further improve your skills by testing for certifications in the cybersecurity industry. Obtaining these qualifications could demonstrate that you have focused on a specific set of white hat hacking skills, or a certain type of security system, and that you know those well. Some of the classes offered at ITT Tech for the Information Systems and Cybersecurity bachelor's degree include:

- Cybercrime Forensics
- Hacking and Countermeasures
- Information Technology Infrastructure Security
- Network Communications Infrastructure
- Risk Management in Information Technology Security
- Security Auditing for Compliance
- Security for Web Applications and Social Networking
- Security Issues in Legal Context
- Security Policies and Implementation

These classes focus more on the security in a company as a whole, and the impact security has on the way a company works. With this level of education, your job could include being responsible for the security and operation of all, or very large pieces, of a company's computer systems, possibly in multiple locations or even countries. You could also work for a cybersecurity firm, bank, or other large organization that has a need for higher levels of security than the average company. It is possible you may manage people in the department you work in, and be responsible for reporting the status of how systems are working and planning the improvements in those systems. This could include budgeting for the labor, materials, and equipment. If you like the big picture as much or more than very detailed hands-on work, this may be a degree for you.

# THE MASTER'S DEGREE

Master's degree programs offer the chance to further enhance your skills and learn new ones. For people interested in white hat hacking, this often means specializing in a particular area of cybersecurity. The classes for a master's program will be much like that of the bachelor's, but more advanced, and will often focus specifically on certain topics. The length of time it will take you to finish the master's program will vary depending on whether you enroll in full-time or part-time courses. Full-time courses require more credits per semester than part-time, and you usually graduate in about two years. Part-time courses take longer to complete, but many people choose this route because it allows them to continue working. Many people will pursue master's degrees after having worked in the IT industry for a while.

This level of education will often lead to high-level jobs with government agencies, such as the Department of Homeland Security and the National Security Agency, or large international financial firms, such as credit card companies or investment firms.

Some white hat jobs that typically require a master's degree include chief security officer, cybersecurity manager or administrator, cybersecurity architect, cryptographer/ cryptologist, and secure software assurance engineer. People in positions such as these will likely lead departments of employees, and will have a high degree of responsibility for the security of the company in which they work. In fact, they may hold some of the top leadership positions in their field.

# PH.D.

A Ph.D. is the highest level of education offered. It is usually designed to teach the skills of the industry to others at colleges or consulting firms. It is also a foundation that you can use to begin a career in researching all areas of cybersecurity, and plan for the future needs of the industry as a whole.

People who attain this degree will often become college professors, think-tank members, and published scientists in the area of cybersecurity. This level of education is usually earned later in your career. It does not necessarily involve any hands-on work or direct contact with the technologies related to computer systems, but it is often chosen by people who have a desire to teach others what they know.

# CERTIFIED ETHICAL HACKER

Where a degree in cybersecurity or a similar field will prepare you for a career in white hat hacking, different certifications are offered to provide detailed training in methods and techniques used by white hat hackers. Although some degree programs will include similar training, certifications are separate from a regular college degree and could be taken by anyone. There are several security certifications offered by many different organizations. One example is the Certified Ethical Hacker (CEH) certificate.

The CEH is offered through the International Council of E-Commerce Consultants (EC-Council), an organization that certifies individuals in different levels of security and **e-business**. An e-business is any business function that uses the Internet and cybersecurity skills. The EC-Council certificate in ethical hacking, according to the organization's website, is the most advanced ethical hacking certificate in the world.

The CEH exam is made up of several sections that cover designing and investigating systems, security testing, how to report and share your findings, ethics, proper use of tools, and testing procedures. This certification will teach you to use the tools and techniques of a regular hacker, but for legal purposes. Having this certification shows employers and law enforcement that you are trained in the proper use of these tools.

The CEH has some requirements in order to qualify to take the test. If you have not completed a degree program in cybersecurity or have not had some work experience in a related field, you are required to first take the Council's training courses, which teach the certification material. You can purchase a textbook or exam guide that covers the material in the test. The test, which is timed, usually requires a fee. The CEH allows a person four hours to take the test, and depending on the version, there are about 125 questions. Tests are held at an approved testing center, which means they may be located in another city. Since technology changes very quickly, your certificate will eventually expire, and you will need to recertify at that time. Typically, this can be from two to five years.

Working with law enforcement can be a large part of a job in white hat hacking.

Similar certifications from other companies include:

• GIAC Certified Penetration Tester (GPEN), which is offered by Global Information Assurance Certification (GIAC)

• OSSTMM Professional Security Expert Accredited Certification (OPSE), offered by the Institute for Security and Open Methodologies (ISECOM)

Certified Network Defense Architect (CNDA) offers a certification course like the CEH, but it is designed solely for employees of the United States government. Only people in certain government jobs are eligible to test for this certification. The content, though, is very similar to the CEH.

Military experience can be valuable and opens doors to opportunities.

# THE MILITARY

Being involved in the military can be a huge advantage in any technology field, especially security. The United States military operates incredibly large, advanced networks worldwide, many of which need to be secured at a higher level than any of the other industries. The government and military maintain an incredible amount of digital records, many requiring a secure storage place. More importantly, when the success of a military operation, defending our citizens, and the safety of our soldiers or even the life of the president are at stake, security is a huge concern.

The military offers options to pursue all of the different educational paths discussed here, and may help or fully pay

# Elite Hackers

The U.S. military has assembled an elite group of white hats to help protect the networks of the U.S. Department of Defense (DoD). Because the DoD has been the target of more than 75,000 intrusion attempts, the creation of such a group was deemed necessary. This white hat team is considered the most elite hacker group ever assembled for the purposes of security. After 9/11, and due to the increased potential for terrorist attacks, the government has made it a priority to seek the best white hats in the business and task them with creating a secure homeland. This hacker team is part of a super-secret, multimillion-dollar weapons program that may be ready to launch bloodless cyberwar against enemy networks—from electric grids to telephone nets.

If the present is any indication of the future, there will likely be many opportunities for skilled, ethical-minded hackers to work to protect the systems of government agencies and the military.

Highly skilled military white hats are key in the modern battlefield and of homeland defense.

Staying current with high-tech security means constantly learning new methods and best practices.

for your degree or training depending on the security field and military branch you enter. Military employees are also often some of the first to explore and use new technologies.

# ON YOUR OWN

There are less formal ways of learning, too, which can often make a big difference. Self-study and experimentation is a huge part of any technology career. Take the time to find resources in books, online, and by talking to other people. They will help you learn more about your desired career as a white hat hacker.

# WHAT'S NEXT?

Once you are educated in white hat skills, there are many different career paths you can take. The government and military are huge employers in the cybersecurity industry. Organizations such as the CIA, FBI, and the DoD all use ethical hackers to test their systems. Most large companies have a security team to monitor and test their internal systems, as well as the systems that they connect to at other companies.

You could take a job as a consultant who travels to different companies throughout the world to provide testing services. This is quite common because even larger corporations with their own cybersecurity professionals are sometimes required to have their testing verified by another company to prove that they are properly testing and reporting their results.

## NOTABLE WHITE HATS

Today there are many white hat hackers, some new, some old, who have made a name. Some have started out on the dark side, but eventually saw the light. These are a few who have an interesting story to tell.

### KEVIN POULSEN

Kevin Poulsen worked for Stanford Research Institute (SRI) International, a research firm dealing in robotics, computing, and chemistry. By night he made a hobby out of manipulating phone

Kevin Poulsen was a well-known hacker turned technology journalist.

systems for his benefit. It is claimed, but unconfirmed, that he once hacked ARPANET. He went underground in 1989 after the FBI began investigating him. When he was featured on NBC's *Unsolved Mysteries,* the show's telephone lines crashed.

His most famous hack was taking control of all of the phone lines for radio station KIIS-FM in Los Angeles because he wanted to be the 102nd caller to win a Porsche 944 S2.

Poulsen has since had a legitimate career as a white hat hacker and journalist. He also co-developed a program to allow secure communication between journalists and their confidential sources. Poulsen, in more recent times, has done work on a social media site tackling sex offenders. He currently is a senior editor for *Wired* magazine.

Tsutomu Shimomura watched Mitnick's activities through logs and computer records.

# TSUTOMU SHIMOMURA

Tsutomu Shimomura is most famous for helping FBI agents catch Kevin Mitnick. Although never a criminal, he was a very capable white hat. One of the ways Shimomura used to find Mitnick was tracking his cell phone signal. He also studied logs and records of the computers Mitnick was connected to, and read messages and notes to other people with whom Mitnick was working. Having the evidence they needed, and a way to find him, the FBI eventually arrested Mitnick. Shimomura is currently CEO and CTO of Neofocal Systems, a company that manufactures LED controller microchips.

# KEVIN MITNICK

As you have already read, Mitnick has been charged with several crimes. His black hat activities involved phone-system hacking such as learning ways to place free international calls and hacking voicemail boxes.

Mitnick now owns the computer security firm Mitnick Security Consulting LLC. The organization focuses on social engineering, website application security, and network penetration. He also operates the security training company KnowBe4, which specializes in teaching the prevention of security problems he once caused.

Kevin Mitnick now helps companies avoid the problems that he mastered.

Some of the best white hat tools can fit on a single DVD.

# 3 WHAT A WHITE HAT DOES

## TOOLS OF THE TRADE

Before going into detail about a day in the life of a white hat hacker, you have to know what tools are used on the job. Every job has its essential tools, and the more specialized the job is, the more unique the tools are. For example, many people own a wrench, you can buy one at any hardware store. However, a firefighter carries a hydrant wrench, specifically built to remove the cover on a fire hydrant and open the valve that allows water to flow through the hose. You won't find one at the hardware store. White hat hacking is no different. Almost everyone uses a computer, but your computer is nothing like that of a white hat hacker's. There are some basic tools that any white hat hacker needs. Proper use of these tools is important; some can cause real damage to the systems you are testing.

> ❝ ❞
> *Almost everyone uses*
> *a computer, but your*
> *computer is nothing like*
> *a white hat hacker's.*
> JONATHAN SMITH

## TIGER BOX

A tiger box is a computer—usually a laptop—that holds many of the different tools a white hat hacker uses. Some of the software on it may be illegal in some areas, and leaving the country with some of them may also be a federal offense. (Laws may vary from place to place.) Many of these software programs do not run on the same operating system, so it will have multiple versions installed on it, such as Linux, Windows, and Mac OS, possibly different versions of each. Some of the tools and packages of tools include the following.

### ICMP

Internet Control Message Protocol (ICMP) is a set of tools used every day by many IT professionals, and by equipment to check basic information about the status of a network. One of the tools in this set is Ping, which is used to confirm that a computer or piece of equipment is connected to the network and responding by asking the computer if it is there. Another is PingPath, which is like Ping, but it will detail the path the signal took to reach the computer on the network by providing a visual of each step. Monitoring these tools for long periods can tell you when computers are turned on and off, if they are moved, and much more. This is often unnoticed on a computer network. It is much like ringing someone's doorbell and then running down the street.

# NMAP

Nmap is another basic tool used to collect information. A network port scanner, Nmap is used to discover hosts and services on a computer network, thus creating a "map" of the network. To accomplish its goal, Nmap sends specially crafted packets to the target host and then analyzes the responses. It does this by sending a request to every **IP address**. The type of response received indicates whether the port is used and can therefore be probed further for weakness.

Nmap does not generally cause any damage or interruption, but it can be detected by some computer security systems. Using Nmap on a computer network is much like walking down the street and stopping at every house, looking in every window. Then looking at the color of the house, the shape and size, and then knocking on every window and door and asking the names of everyone who lives inside and what they do for a living, and you are taking notes the whole time. Doing this at one or two houses in a neighborhood may not look suspicious, but if you do this to an entire block, you will eventually draw attention.

# NESSUS VULNERABILITY SCANNER

Nessus is a scanning tool designed to automate the testing and discovery of known security problems. Typically someone, whether a hacker group, a security company, or a researcher, discovers a specific way to violate the security of a software product. For example, if you never download updates to your computer, your individual PC would appear on an alert screen because Nessus has detected "missing updates." Nessus can also detect signs of viruses, sensitive and personal information that is not secure, and even check mobile devices such as tablets and phones. This is also easy to spot with security software. Imagine walking down that same street, and while peeking in windows you are also asking if your neighbor is sick, and whether it would be easy to steal their TV! People will take notice of that very quickly, and that kind of behavior on a computer network stands out just as easily.

# TOOL PACKAGES

There are packages of tools available that compile many of the most popular tools into a single software package. By bundling the tools into a single DVD that can be used to boot your laptop, it places everything you need at your fingertips.

## METASPLOIT

Metasploit is a set of tools that runs in one program, and can be used to test for specific problems in computers. For instance, if you run the Nessus scanner it will provide a list of problems detected. By using Metasploit, you can test to see if what the scanner found really is a problem. The tools in Metasploit are designed to try and mimic what a hacker will do to take advantage of a weakness. This is called an exploit. There are currently more than 2,500 exploits in the Metasploit database. Some of these exploits will collect passwords, allow someone to access a computer without a username or password, and even copy information from a computer.

Some of the worst exploits can delete important system files or ruin user accounts and passwords, or even shut down a computer altogether. This is one of the tools that requires care. The exploits that do damage can be used to test solutions to those problems on a test system. Using them on a real production system could cause permanent damage.

## BACKTRACK

Backtrack is a large collection of tools that includes much of what is already listed here, and more. Backtrack runs in the Linux operating system and includes tools for computer forensics.

Testing live websites or systems can break them, sometimes permanently.

These are methods of investigating and keeping information about a computer for evidence, to help determine who has accessed files on a computer and when. It also includes tools to test phone, Wi-Fi, and Bluetooth security problems. The Backtrack tools are no longer being developed, but are still useful and great for learners and professionals. It has been replaced by Kali Linux, a full operating system that includes all the tools from Backtrack and more.

## HONEYPOT

Part of testing security is knowing what to look for, where it's coming from, and how it's done. A honeypot—a computer or piece of equipment that is made to look attractive to a hacker—does just that. It might be part of an e-mail system, or a file that holds customer addresses, or some similar role in your company. On the outside it looks perfectly normal, but perhaps it has an artificial

A honeypot is a sweet and tempting trap to learn about hackers' activities.

security flaw that makes it slightly easier to get into than normal. It should store fake information but should be made to look as real as possible. A honeypot contains software to monitor what is being done to the computer. It might also be able to track the hacker's path.

After black hat hackers discover the honeypot, explore it, and likely attack it, the white hat hacker can look at the system's logs and other equipment to determine how the hacker accessed it or whether or not the methods they used were successful. It is possible that the honeypot might be crippled or infected with a virus the hacker installed. It is also possible the hacker's equipment might have caught a virus. Some honeypots will infect the attacker in the hope of identifying the hacker if they return later.

# PENETRATION TESTING

A penetration test is used to determine where the weaknesses in a network or a building are located. Using all of the tools discussed, a white hat will attempt to poke holes and find cracks in a system's security to highlight areas that should be fixed. It can also be a way of showing that security holes have already been fixed. When hired to perform a penetration test, you or your company will sign a contract that sets rules and guidelines for testing. One of the terms included in this contract is permission for the tester to run the test. This is very important because it will give the tester proof that he or she was allowed to use the tools they have in case anyone ever claims the work was done maliciously.

Depending on the type of penetration test, it might also list what kinds of tests are allowed to run, what systems can be tested, or what should be avoided. This can be for many reasons. Many penetration tests are designed to check systems against a certain type of threat, or for certain guidelines. These guidelines may only require that certain systems be tested and only certain types of tests need to be run.

The contract will also describe what your responsibility is if something goes wrong during the test or if something gets ruined. In many cases, the tester may write in the contract that they are not responsible if the tests ruin equipment or cause harm to the company. The company whose system is being tested will usually want the tester to agree not to share what they tested, what the results were, or any other information they learned while conducting the test. This is important for security reasons. If you find a problem with security in a large company that needs to be fixed, and it gets leaked to the public, the company can quickly become a target.

# TESTING METHODS

In addition to knowing the tools, white hat hackers must also be familiarized with different testing methods. Following are some examples.

## BLACK BOX

Black box security testing is a method where the tester has little or no real knowledge of the system being tested. It is designed to mimic real-world scenarios where an external hacker is not likely to have any in-depth knowledge of the company he or she is hacking, or its systems. The tester may need to try several different approaches to running the same test, and at different times, to secure a good result.

The company may not tell its staff that the test is occurring. This means the internal security staff may try **countermeasures** against the attack. Countermeasures are designed to prevent or stop an attack, and could stop or fool the test. Because of this, black box testing can be hit or miss. It is possible that some systems may never be tested if they are never found. This method will also usually take much more time, and will show how the security responds to random attacks.

## WHITE BOX

In a white box test the tester is provided much more information about the types of equipment in the network, and may be given designs and other instructions on how the system works. The tester may also be able to meet with security and technical staff to ask questions and get more details about the system. They may even be given specific instructions on what to test.

Knowing what is inside the system, the tester can select tools and techniques that are more system specific. This is all done to

Red team vs. blue team exercises can be as complicated as a chess match.

make it easier to focus the testing on specific areas, or so nothing is missed. A white box test is very thorough, but does not reflect the real world if it is an outside attack. Of course, not every attack starts on the outside. An upset employee or even a virus could initiate an attack from the inside. White box testing can be very useful in determining how systems react to a hack that comes from inside.

## RED TEAM VS. BLUE TEAM

The red team vs. blue team hacking test involves a group of white hats (called the red or tiger team) on one side who are actively hacking a company, or possibly the government, for testing. On the other side is another group of white hats (called the blue team) trying to defend the systems being hacked. This type of testing allows an organization to identify its security vulnerabilities and how to protect itself while being hacked.

This could be done in real life using all of the tools, equipment, and staff that would normally be involved in a penetration test. A panel could also address it during a roundtable discussion, or map out a strategy on a whiteboard. Sometimes it is done all three ways, using the table exercise as a practice run. This can be done repeatedly, even with the teams switching sides.

# JOBS AND ROLES OF A WHITE HAT

The job description and role of a white hack hacker comes in many shapes and forms. The training that leads to being a white hat touches many different areas of IT, and the job titles can be diverse. One thing to be careful of in any technology field is interpreting the job titles. Words such as "specialist," "analyst," and "engineer" can mean very different things at different companies. It is also important to know that you can't always determine someone's level of experience with these titles. When looking for work or exploring jobs, ask specific questions about the expected responsibilities and tasks. Being a white hat hacker is a somewhat general term; the actual title will vary greatly. The job titles listed below are all used by white hat hackers:

- Penetration Tester
- Certified Ethical Hacker
- Cybersecurity Analyst
- Applications Security Specialist
- Network Security Specialist
- Web Security Specialist

These positions may be offered as a full-time job at a medium- to large-sized company. They could also be available at consulting firms hired by organizations to perform security-related work.

Many security consultants also have a wide variety of skills. Working for a consulting firm can lead to opportunities of specializing in specific areas of security, and a consultant (or freelancer) may be contracted for those specific skills on a regular basis. When working as a freelancer, you have the flexibility to take on as many or as few assignments as you like. Most consultants are very busy and frequently work much longer hours than those in a typical workweek.

# DIARY OF A WHITE HAT HACKER

You have now learned a lot about white hat hacking and what the job entails. What really goes on during a white hat's workday? Take this as an example.

Every morning, Andy B., a professional white hat hacker, goes to work just like countless others. Wearing business casual clothes and a smile, he breezes past security and into his office, sits at his desk, and logs on at a computer terminal. Today, Andy has been tasked to perform a black box test for Aardvark Pharmaceuticals (a fictional company).

Andy reads the rules of his contract, and brushes up on the client's expectations. Then, he goes to Aardvark to begin his assignment. Aardvark has three buildings, an office, a garage for delivery trucks, and a warehouse. The company created a new website and is expanding its offices. They want to ensure their new website is secure, and have brought Andy in as a consultant. Andy is allowed to hack anything he can get access to, which includes doors, safes, computers, and any other company asset. He is told not to go into the warehouse where all of the ready-to-ship products are stored. Aardvark has a new, closely guarded piece of equipment there, one considered a trade secret. Andy's activities are a secret to most of the company employees. Aardvark's security team will contact law enforcement if a trespasser is found.

Andy browses a few public records to confirm Aardvark's website statistics. This goes quickly. He has a list of the computers that hold Aardvark's websites. After looking over the website, everything seems normal, except a link in the corner that reads "Employee Portal."

He begins by using the Nessus scanner to check those servers for vulnerabilities. While Nessus scans the website, Andy decides to take a walk down the street. He sees a few people leave, one of who is wearing an Aardvark jacket. He follows them closely enough so that he appears to be part of the group. As they approach the back door he sees a group of people standing outside. They welcome him. Andy laughs at a few jokes being told, and after a few minutes people head back inside. He tailgates them.

Some tactics used by hackers include following people into usually inaccessible areas.

Andy walks down a hall to a small office area; an employee is getting up. Trying not to draw attention, he stops to read a sign on a corkboard. As that employee walks past, Andy quickly sits at the empty desk.

White Hat Hacking

This employee's username is in the box on the screen. Andy jots it down on a notepad and stuffs it in his pocket. Next he sees a phone list on the side of the desk and uses his camera to take a quick picture. Andy now has a username for Aardvark's systems. Time to get back to the office.

The scan has confirmed that the main website is up to date and well secured. Although no vulnerabilities appear on the scan, there is a flag on the link to the Employee Portal. It is a broken link, meaning that it cannot be connected to from the outside. It probably only works from inside the company buildings, or on computers connected to the internal network. This signals to Andy that whatever is on the other side of that link might be important or private since it is not supposed to be seen from the outside of the company. He wants to see if he can hack into that link without being in an Aardvark building.

Andy noticed employee Jim on his fake Twitter account. Jim is sending tweets about how boring it is on the late shift at the warehouse. Andy knows he can't go to the warehouse, but he can go to the garage where the trucks are located. It would be hard to risk going back in, but Andy has an idea. He grabs his phone and checks the list. Bill is at extension 317—that could mean he is on the third floor. Andy calls the main number for Aardvark and presses 317. "This is Bill," a voice announces.

Andy tells Bill, "I'm the new guy here." Andy tells Bill that he is on the second floor waiting in the conference room for a meeting with his new boss and can't get on the Wi-Fi. Bill, duped, is happy to help Andy get connected. "Thanks, Bill! You're a lifesaver," says Andy. It's about 4 p.m. It might be a long night.

At nine o'clock, Andy grabs his laptop and stuffs it into his bag. After walking a few blocks, he sees the warehouse. Large fences surround the building, and security guards are on alert. Trucks are coming and going from the garage across the street.

Andy takes a seat at the picnic table outside the door. The garage has access to the Aardvark internal Wi-Fi. After connecting with the password Bill gave him earlier, he loads his Internet browser. The Employee Portal link works now! He is being asked for a username and password. He has the username "tim2." Tim is probably the user's name, and the number is likely in sequence depending on the number of employees named Tim. Andy rechecks the phone list. Sure enough, two are named Tim, but there is only one Bill. That makes Bill "bill1." Andy starts his scanners again, and this time adds a password-guessing tool. There are several combinations, and it will take time. Andy leaves the laptop under a bush and goes for a walk. He stops back at about 4:17 a.m. The battery is about to die, but that's OK. He has to get back to the office and check his results.

Before he lays down for a nap, he plugs in the laptop and BOOM—the password for bill1, "lion," has been uncovered! Andy knows he could access a lot of secure information using Bill's account. He is in the accounting department after all, and they handle money, but that is not why Andy is here. As a white hat, he has no need to access Bill's account. He only needs to know that it was easily cracked. Andy has checked the website using a black box test inside and out without breaking the rules. He is ready to report his findings to Aardvark Pharmaceuticals.

Because Andy is a white hat, he will use his skills to improve Aardvark's security by exposing vulnerabilities before malicious hackers cause damage. Other types of hackers include blue hat hackers and gray hat hackers. Blue hat hackers are security professionals who are invited by Microsoft to expose vulnerabilities in Windows products. Gray hat hackers are hackers who perform both malicious activities and helpful ones.

# REPORTING

In the end, everything needs to be documented and reported back to the client. This report should be professionally written, and include several different sections. A summary will provide a brief overview of the findings and recommendations. This is for the leadership of the company you are testing for, and is meant to give a very quick explanation of your findings.

Giving detailed information and keeping accurate records is a key part of white hat hacking.

The report will also include the types of tests performed, where they were performed, and who performed them. A timeline will also detail events from start to finish throughout the entire testing process. The report should include a list of the vulnerabilities detected, as well as recommendations to repair them.

## WHO DOES THIS?

From local IT shops to large international security firms, there are many companies that provide security-testing services. They will employ several white hats holding various certifications. This way they can offer services to many different types of companies.

# White Hat Lite

**N**ot all white hats perform white hat hacking as their main job. You will find that other IT professions are just as concerned about security, and will often study the ways of the white hats to learn how to better secure their own networks.

Website and mobile developers are two professions with a lot of exposure to user information requiring security measures. Joe Wetzel, a professional mobile and web developer, shared that in the early days, development methods were not always secure. "I think a lot of us that were doing development didn't know best practices because they didn't exist." This included a lack of encryption. Programmers were using methods that could make private information easy to access. Security testing was not common.

Joe started to gain an interest in white hat hacking methods early in his career because he "realized that web applications have vulnerabilities." He saw the work that he and his colleagues were doing and realized that there were no best practices for security. There were simply too many vulnerabilities.

Security tools are improving; a default option in the software that promotes security is one example. Programmers now use tools in their day-to-day jobs that help catch attempted hacks that are common, such as trying to replace information on a website. Computers also include automated tools that help find security problems with any code you publish to a website or app. It has become important to protect the people who use their apps, and security teams now have an expectation that code will be secure.

> *In the early days I think a lot of us that were doing development didn't know best practices because they didn't exist.*
>
> JOE WETZEL, PROFESSIONAL MOBILE AND WEBSITE DEVELOPER

Some organizations are creating security councils to discuss security concerns among the different areas of IT. Schools and businesses select IT representatives as well as non-technical staff for these committees. This helps raise awareness among the different IT roles about what each is doing to promote security. All of these people wear a white hat in hopes of making the company or school a safer place. Does your school have a committee such as this?

Programmers try to improve their security practices by testing and sharing best practices.

Coalfire Systems Inc. is an independent IT audit and compliance firm with offices in many major U.S. cities. Coalfire specializes in security and testing services. They have been in business since 2001, and work in many different industries such as financial services, health care, hospitality, and higher education. Coalfire doesn't just offer testing services, they also offer advice on how to manage security for an organization as a whole.

RedSpin Inc. is a little different. They are more specialized, offering mostly penetration testing and software testing services. They also offer social engineering awareness services and security training. Founded in 2000, they also serve a wide range of industries.

There are many similar companies all over the world. Most of them will provide security updates and articles about current threats on their websites. Most will include a blog or forum on their website for users to read about and discuss what is going on in the security industry.

Now that you know what it's like to be a white hat hacker, and how to make sure you get the right education for the type of career you want, you're probably wondering how much money white hat hackers earn. To answer this, we have to discuss salaries, benefits, and what each level of career means.

Entering the business world can be scary, but it also means you can use the skills you have developed.

# 4 PERKS, PAY, PROS, AND CONS

## WHAT'S IN IT FOR ME?

Enjoying your work is an important part of why you choose a particular career path. However, the compensation and benefits for doing that job are just as important to most people. IT-related careers are some of the higher paying jobs available. Demand for security professionals is growing constantly, and white hat hacking is no exception.

According to the InfoSec Institute, in 2014, the average salary for a Certified Ethical Hacker was about $71,000 per year, with some people making as much as $132,000. As with many jobs, pay will be different based on experience and geographic location. According to the United States Department of Labor, New York City has the highest average salary of white hat hackers, followed by California. Full-time jobs in cybersecurity will almost always carry benefits such as health insurance, retirement plans, and tuition reimbursement, for taking classes or certifications.

> ## *In general, the more education or training a security job requires, the more it will pay.*
> JONATHAN SMITH

In general, the more education or training a security job requires, the more it will pay.

There are many different titles for a white hat hacker. A security administrator position is often entry-level, followed by a security analyst, security manager, and security director. As you review job postings, each has a slightly higher average salary than the last. Along with the salary, the level of experience and responsibility will also increase. As a security analyst you are often working in a team, often helping the higher-level positions achieve their goals. Typically this job will have a lower salary. In contrast, a director level position is usually held by just one person in each department, and pays very well. A director leads the department and is held responsible for its collective performance. When exploring these types of jobs, consider what level of stress you can handle, and how much time you want to spend at work.

## YOUR CAREER PATH

Part of plotting a career path in cybersecurity is learning the newest tricks and tools. Getting to know other people in your industry can be equally important. Sharing ideas was a big part of

Getting involved in professional groups is a wonderful way to learn and share ideas.

what hacking was originally about: the freedom of information. There are different clubs and groups that IT professionals can belong to, which meet for sharing ideas and viewing presentations on new and upcoming technology.

One of these groups is the Association of Information Technology Professionals. This association has student chapters in many colleges across the United States, and hosts various local, regional, and national events. Specific to the security-related IT professions, the Information Systems Security Association (ISSA) is an international association that holds similar events.

According to a 2014 survey published by the San Diego Region Regional Economic Development Corporation, cybersecurity firms were expected to grow by more than 10 percent over the next year. Cybersecurity-related jobs in the San Diego area are expected to grow more than 20 percent in the next year. This is a common trend in other areas of the country as well.

Rules and regulations over personal information are becoming tighter. The number of companies and computer systems that request your information or that have desirable information grows and changes all the time. For example, you may have a cell phone that stores your passwords for apps that allows you to make purchases with your parent's credit card. Just a few years ago that wasn't even an option. New techniques had to be worked through to make that safe, and sometimes that takes new people to create new ideas. Many industry analysts feel this trend will continue to grow in the United States for years to come. The U.S. Bureau of Labor Statistics published that the job growth for an information security analyst is expected to be 37 percent from 2012 to 2022 across the entire country. This means that for every 100 jobs in 2012, they expect to see 137 jobs in 2022. That is much higher than the average for job availability increase.

As you have read, there are several educational options as well as job choices for a career in cybersecurity. Once in a job, the direction you take will depend on the types of projects you are assigned, what interests you, and changes in the direction of the industry. It is possible you can start in a company as an entry-level or middle-level employee and work your way to the top.

It is very common to change employers from time to time in technology jobs, especially as you develop new skills or interests. It is also possible that you will start in a certain area of cybersecurity and work your way into a career that has less and less to do with security. Some of the original white hats (and black hats) are still working as consultants but many have found opportunities teaching and training upcoming white hats as well as company leaders and business owners. Some have even moved into other technical and non-technical areas, such as journalism. There are many tech-related magazines, podcasts, and blogs that have hired former white and black hats. You could also find work as a college professor. Like many other IT-related jobs, the possibilities are endless.

> *"*
> *"*
>
> *It is very common to change employers from time to time in technology jobs, especially as you develop new skills or interests.*
>
> JONATHAN SMITH

# DOING IT YOURSELF

Besides income from a regular job, many white hats will find freelance work to make extra money. There are some people who write programming code by day and do freelance security work at night, and vice versa. Many major companies have programs called a "bug bounty." These companies pay white and gray hats to find bugs and weaknesses in their systems. The pay will vary depending on the type of work you're asked to do and the seriousness of a possible hack. Some bounties are restricted to testing against an alternate system that will not interrupt the company's business activity. Also, for any work you do you will need to provide proof of the vulnerabilities you find and written steps detailing the process. Some companies will pay thousands of dollars for your findings.

If you choose to be a freelance white hat instead of taking a job with a company, there is plenty of work. The hacking community has a long history of self-education and freethinking, that is, living

There are many opportunities to make a good living in computer security.

and thinking "outside the box." You are also better equipped to land projects that lead you down the career you want to go into, whereas working with a company sometimes means going in the direction they want to go instead. There are websites and groups set up to help you find work, such as freelancer.com. This kind of work is sometimes called contract work. You are hired for a certain period of time to perform a certain task or set of tasks. It is possible that working a contract could lead to a permanent full-time job as well. Sometimes new or expanding companies will hire someone on a contract basis first, and then as full-time if they need an additional person to do a specific job.

In some cases you can work several contracts at once, although some companies don't allow you to be involved in other related projects at the same time. More contracts can lead to more pay than a regular job; however, the companies you work for will

White Hat Hacking

not offer benefits such as health insurance that may cost more to get on your own than if it was offered by a full-time employer. You are also going to have to pay to educate yourself in the newest tools and methods.

# THE GOOD AND THE BAD

Being a white hat hacker offers a lot of flexibility. Depending on how you want to live and work, you could travel extensively, which would all be paid for by your clients or employer. Large corporations and consulting companies may often require travel as part of the job; however, a lot of IT work can be done remotely, depending on the kind of testing you are doing and the expectations of your employer. In fact, you could stay in one place and work remotely for many white hat jobs, especially those who test software.

Make sure everyone agrees with and understands the expectations when freelancing.

Being a white hat hacker carries a lot of responsibility along with some risk. Consequences for making mistakes can be drastic if you damage someone's systems or cause an unexpected disruption. It is important that if you are a freelance white hat you have legal representation to review your contracts and help you understand the conditions you agree to when you take a job.

White hats often get to see and learn about new technology before it is released to the public. Mobile devices, for example, often go through testing for safety, FCC compliance, and security before being announced to the public officially. Many online games are given

# White Hat Fun!

The types of people who gravitate to jobs in white hat hacking have a tendency to be those who like to tinker, invent, and create. They will see something and want to know what makes it tick, and if something different can be done, they want to be the ones who do that. "For me it was about thinking differently," Joe Wetzel says. White hats and black hats in the early days often had hobbies like building and repairing Ham Radios. Sometimes they would modify them to work on channels restricted to police and fire departments. Another popular hobby is picking locks (yes, sometimes just for fun) and altering audio-video equipment.

Today, it is not much different, just more advanced. Creating electronic toys and gadgets from kits and spare parts is a common hobby of white hat hackers. Bug Bots, which are little robotic bugs that can interact with people and other bugs like real insects by responding to sounds, being touched, or coming close to a wall, are one example. You will also find that many white hat hackers are Lego fans who enjoy working with the Mindstorm Legos, creating and programming small robots. A little more advanced is the Raspberry Pi, a credit card-sized computer that can be plugged in to a monitor and programmed to do many different things with sound, video, and other tools. It can even interact with the outside world, such as developing a sensor to tell when the fridge is opened.

Even recycling older electronics can be fun. Joe Wetzel, for example, created a project with an old iPad. He mounted the iPad in the glass window on his office door and wrote an app that listens to the door. When someone knocked on the door, it could take a picture with the iPad camera and show it to him. If the person knocked again within a few seconds, it would Tweet the photo.

Robots, like this Lego Mindstorm robot, and electronics are common hobbies for white hats.

Many white hats are also gamers, so it is not uncommon to find them at energy-drink-fueled LAN parties where people bring their PC or console games to play with others in the same place on a computer network. Such events are often hosted by schools or computer clubs.

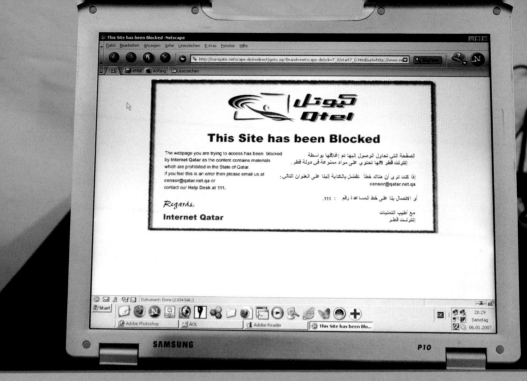

Working in secure environments can mean putting up with heavy restrictions.

to white hats to uncover possible weaknesses before they are sold to the public.

Today cybersecurity is a big deal. It is always in the news and may stay that way for a long time. Because of this, many security departments are very well funded, and pay higher than average. This means that today's cybersecurity professionals can have access to the latest tools and training, and are encouraged to keep on top of the changes. Not all jobs are this way. Many companies, however, are encouraging people to do more work with fewer tools, which means cutting back.

In some cases, being in a high-security environment can be less than desirable. Working in a government agency that has many restrictions means you may have to use outdated tools and even work on older computers. Operating systems are often easier to secure when they have been around and tested for a long time.

However, using the most up-to-date technology is always an advantage. If you are using Firefox or Chrome at home with tons of extensions and add-ins, you may find that you will have to relearn an older version of Internet Explorer at work.

Even working at a company that has a high-security area, such as credit card processing, can be challenging. Some of these systems require you to document when and why you used them, and check out a username and password from your security department. You may even be restricted to accessing the systems at certain times.

Sometimes gray hat hackers, hackers who perform the same tests as white hat hackers but without informing or getting permission from the company, can give white hats a bad name and can be regarded as just as dangerous as black hat hackers. Often gray hats do not mean any harm, but since they do not have permission or a contract to perform testing, they can be subject to the same legal punishments as a black hat. Some gray hats run tests against companies in hopes that the company will then hire them to fix problems they have found. Some of them have been arrested or threatened with legal action for doing so. Many true white hats object to this for many reasons. One, it is unethical to do the testing without permission. Besides, can you trust what a stranger is telling you, especially when they are looking for a payment to fix something you didn't even know was wrong? It is worth knowing that gray hats do sometimes find legitimate issues about which manufacturers of a product or software may be unaware. In response, many companies have started special programs, such as the bug bounty, to guide gray hats finding these issues in a controlled way that requires a tester to follow certain guidelines.

# WHERE TO GO FROM HERE

At the back of this book are resources you can use to discover more about white hat hacking. They will help you further explore the topics discussed in this book, but don't stop there.

Share what you have learned, and explore your opportunities!

Ask your teachers, parents, or even the IT people at your school about their job and how it relates to white hat hacking. Your school may even have a cybersecurity professional on staff right now who might have stories to share or who could help you find out how your school handles security.

Consider giving a presentation on white hat ideas for your speech class. You might be able to find a local security company that could give a presentation at your school for career day. Check to see if your school has a computer or electronics club. Many of them may also be interested in what you read about in this book. Most of all, keep asking questions. A white hat wants to know how and why, and is not happy until they get an answer!

# GLOSSARY

**black hat hacker**  Someone who would use one of many tools or techniques to gain access to another person's secured information. Black hat hacking is illegal.

**computer forensics**  The process of investigating, analyzing, and gathering evidence from a computer for presentation in a court of law.

**computer fraud**  Using information technology to commit fraud.

**computer logs**  A file that records the events that happen on a computer.

**computer networking**  Connecting computer systems so that they can share information electronically.

**computer viruses**  Programs that cause harm to or copy themselves onto a computer.

**countermeasures**  Software/hardware products or actions that prevent intruders from gaining access to your system.

**database systems**  Usually a large collection of information stored on a computer especially for searching and retrieval.

**e-business**  Any business that makes some or all of its money using Internet technology.

# GLOSSARY

**encryption**  The process of changing information to prevent unauthorized people from accessing it.

**exploit**  A technique or software tool designed to take advantage of a flaw in a computer system.

**HIPAA laws**  The federal Health Insurance Portability and Accountability Act of 1996. The laws define rules for protecting the confidentiality of health care information.

**IP address**  A unique set of numbers assigned to a device on a computer network.

**operating systems**  The main program in a computer that controls the computer and makes it possible for other programs to function.

**PCI DSS**  The Payment Card Industry Data Security Standard is a security standard for organizations that handle credit card information.

**port scanners**  A software application designed to look at a computer and find programs that are listening for other computers to talk to them.

**programming languages**  Languages used to give a machine or computer instructions to complete a task.

**shoulder surfing** Refers to using observation, such as looking over someone's shoulder, to get information.

**sniffers** A computer tool that captures communications between computers and decodes them so you can see the information it holds.

**social engineering** The social procedure of manipulating people into performing actions or giving confidential information.

**systems administrator** A person who is responsible for the configuration and operation of computer systems.

**virtual machines** A software-based imitation of a computer system.

# INTRODUCTION

(1) pg. 5: U.S. Department of Health & Human Services. "Who is Covered by the Privacy Rule." Health Information Privacy. Accessed May 29, 2014. www.hhs.gov/ocr/privacy/hipaa/ understanding/summary/privacysummary.pdf.

# CHAPTER 1

(1) pg. 12: Biggs, John. *Black Hat: Misfits, Criminals, and Scammers in the Internet Age*. Berkeley, CA: Apress, 2004. Pg. 7.

(2) pg. 12: Van Vleck, Tom. "How the Air Force Cracked Multics Security." Multics. Accessed May 5, 2014. www.multicians. org/security.html.

(3) pg. 13: Dalakov, Georgi. "Internet, Birth, and First computer virus of Bob Thomas." History of Computers and Computing. Accessed May 6, 2014. history-computer.com/Internet/ Maturing/Thomas.html.

(4) pg. 14: National Criminal Justice Reference Service. "Comprehensive Crime Control Act of 1984." National Criminal Justice Reference Service. Accessed May 5, 2014. www.ncjrs.gov/pdffiles1/Digitization/123365NCJRS.pdf.

(5) pg. 17: Biggs. *Black Hat: Misfits, Criminals, and Scammers in the Internet Age*. Pg. 59–61.

(6) pg. 18: Venema, Wietse, and Dan Farmer, "Improving the Security of Your Site by Breaking Into It." www.csm.ornl. gov/~dunigan/cracking.html.

(7) pg. 23: Tarnovsky, Christopher. Interview by Dr. Katherine Albrecht. Radio Broadcast, Appleton, WI, May 26, 2009.

## CHAPTER 2

(1) pg. 33: Pearson, Jake, "Inside The Cybersecurity, 'White Hat Hacker' University Network." www.huffingtonpost.com/2013/04/11/cybersecurity-hacker-network-college_n_3064465.html.

(2) pg. 36: Hagerstown Community College. "2012–2013 Catalog." Hagerstown Community College. Accessed May 1, 2014. catalog.hagerstowncc.edu/preview_program.php?catoid=2&poid=243&returnto=82.

(3) pg. 38: "Information Systems and Cybersecurity." ITT Technical Institute. Accessed May 5, 2014. www.itt-tech.edu/teach/list/isc.cfm.

(4) pg. 40: EC-Council. "Ethical Hacking and Countermeasures to Become Certified Ethical Hacker." CEH: Certified Ethical Hacking course from EC-Council. Accessed May 5, 2014. www.eccouncil.org/Certification/certified-ethical-hacker.

(5) pg. 41: EC-Council. "Application Process / Eligibility." Application Process Eligibility. Accessed May 10, 2014. cert.eccouncil.org/application-process-eligibility.html.

(6) pg. 46: DeSantis, Jeanette. "Man Gets Longest Term for Hacker: Computers: Kevin Lee Poulsen, 29, of North Hollywood is ordered jailed for 51 months for rigging telephone lines during radio call-in contests." *Los Angeles Times*. April 11, 1995.

# SOURCE NOTES

## CHAPTER 3

(1) pg. 50: Simpson, Michael T., Kent Backman and James E. Corley. *Hands-on Ethical Hacking and Network Defense*. Boston, MA: Thomson Course Technology, 2013. Pg. 3.

(2) pg. 52: Rapid7. "Vulnerability & Exploit Database | Rapid7." Vulnerability & Exploit Database. Accessed May 1, 2014. www.rapid7.com/db/modules.

(3) pg. 63: Alharbi, Mansour. "Writing a Penetration Testing Report." SANS Institute InfoSec Reading Room. Accessed April 26, 2014. www.sans.org/reading-room/whitepapers/bestprac/writing-penetration-testing-report-33343.

(4) pg. 67: "Coalfire – Independent IT Audit & Compliance for PCI, HIPAA, FISMA, GLBA." Coalfire. Accessed May 12, 2014. www.coalfire.com/Home.

(5) pg. 67: RedSpin. "Penetration Testing Services & Security Audits: Proven Methodology. Exceptional Results." Redspin Penetration Testing, IT Security Assessments, HIPAA. Accessed May 10, 2014. www.redspin.com.

(6) pg. 64: Wetzel. Personal interview.

(7) pg. 65: Wetzel, Joe. Interview by author. Personal interview. Appleton, WI, May 9, 2014.

# CHAPTER 4

(1) pg. 69: U.S. Bureau of Labor Statistics. "Summary." U.S. Bureau of Labor Statistics. Accessed May 11, 2014. www.bls.gov/ooh/computer-and-information-technology/information-security-analysts.htm.

(2) pg. 71: "Cybersecurity Is San Diego's Next Frontier in Rapid Job Growth." Reuters. Accessed May 11, 2014. www.reuters.com/article/2014/03/20/eset-cyber-security-idUSnPn90bQwP+85+PRN20140320.

(3) pg. 72: U.S. Bureau of Labor Statistics. "Summary."

(4) pg. 73: "Bug Bounty." Techopedia. Accessed May 5, 2014. www.techopedia.com/definition/28637/bug-bounty.

(5) pg. 76: Wetzel. Personal interview.

(6) pg. 78: Electronic Frontier Foundation. "A 'Grey Hat' Guide." Electronic Frontier Foundation. Accessed May 12, 2014. www.eff.org/pages/grey-hat-guide.

(7) pg. 78: "Bug Bounty." Techopedia. www.techopedia.com/definition/28637/bug-bounty.

# BOOKS

Basta, Alfred, Nadine Basta, and Mary Brown. *Computer Security and Penetration Testing*. 2nd ed. Stamford, CT: Cengage Learning, 2014.

Cole, Eric, and Ronald L. Krutz. *Network Security Bible*. 2nd ed. Indianapolis, IN: Wiley Publishing, 2009.

McClure, Stuart, and Joel Scambray. *Hacking Exposed: Network Security Secrets & Solutions*. 4th ed. Berkeley, CA: McGraw-Hill/Osborne, 2003.

Simpson, Michael T., Kent Backman, and James E. Corley. *Hands-on Ethical Hacking and Network Defense*. Boston, MA: Thomson Course Technology, 2013.

Wilhelm, Thomas, and Jason Andress. *Ninja Hacking Unconventional Penetration Testing Tactics And Techniques*. Burlington, MA: Syngress/Elsevier, 2011.

# WEBSITES

**Dark Reading**

www.darkreading.com

An e-zine styled website that offers news, articles, cartoons, and other security-related content for all areas of the technology security.

**Hack in the Box**

www.hitb.org

A popular private website dedicated to news and events in the hacking community.

**International Council of Electronic Commerce Consultants**

www.eccouncil.org

The official website of the EC-Council, which offers standards, training, and certification for different cybersecurity roles.

**Security Weekly**

securityweekly.com

An industry website providing podcasts and articles about various information security topics.

Alharbi, Mansour. "Writing a Penetration Testing Report." SANS Institute InfoSec Reading Room. Accessed April 26, 2014. www.sans.org/reading-room/whitepapers/bestprac/writing-penetration-testing-report-33343.

Biggs, John. *Black Hat: Misfits, Criminals, and Scammers in the Internet Age*. Berkeley, CA: Apress, 2004.

"Coalfire - Independent IT Audit & Compliance for PCI, HIPAA, FISMA, GLBA." Coalfire. Accessed May 12, 2014. www.coalfire.com/Home.

Cole, Eric, and Ronald L. Krutz. *Network Security Bible*. 2nd ed. Indianapolis, IN: Wiley Publishing, 2009.

"Cybersecurity Is San Diego's Next Frontier in Rapid Job Growth." Reuters. Accessed May 11, 2014. www.reuters.com/article/2014/03/20/eset-cyber-security-idUSnPn90bQwP+85+PRN20140320.

Dalakov, Georgi. "Internet, Birth, and First computer virus of Bob Thomas." History of Computers and Computing. Accessed May 6, 2014. history-computer.com/Internet/Maturing/Thomas.html.

DeSantis, Jeanette. "Man Gets Longest Term for Hacker: Computers: Kevin Lee Poulsen, 29, of North Hollywood is ordered jailed for 51 months for rigging telephone lines during radio call-in contests." *Los Angeles Times Online*. April 11, 1995. articles.latimes.com/1995-04-11/local/me-53492_1_kevin-lee-poulsen.

EC-Council. "Application Process/Eligibility." Accessed May 10, 2014. cert.eccouncil.org/application-process-eligibility.html.
———"Ethical Hacking and Countermeasures to Become Certified Ethical Hacker." CEH: Certified Ethical Hacking course from EC-Council. Accessed May 5, 2014. www.eccouncil.org/Certification/certified-ethical-hacker.

Fahey, Ryan. "Average Certified Ethical Hacker (C | EH) Salary 2014." InfoSec Institute. Accessed May 11, 2014. resources.infosecinstitute.com/certified-ethical-hacker-salary.

Farmer, Dan, and Wietse Venema. *Forensic Discovery*. Boston, MA: Addison-Wesley, 2005.

Hagerstown Community College. "2012-2013 Catalog." Accessed May 1, 2014. catalog.hagerstowncc.edu/preview_program.php?catoid=2&poid=243&returnto=82.

"IEEE Annals of the History of Computing." *IEEE Computer Society* 27–28 (2005): 74.

ITT Technical Institute. "Information Systems and Cybersecurity." ITT Technical Institute. Accessed May 5, 2014. www.itt-tech.edu/teach/list/isc.cfm.

Kabay, M. E. *A Brief History of Computer Crime*. www.mekabay.com/overviews/history.pdf.

McGuinness, William. "Inside The Cybersecurity, 'White Hat Hacker' University Network." *The Huffington Post Tech*. Accessed May 11, 2014. www.huffingtonpost.com/2013/04/11/cybersecurity-hacker-network-college_n_3064465.html.

# BIBLIOGRAPHY

Mitnick, Kevin D., and William L. Simon. *Ghost in the Wires: My Adventures as the World's Most Wanted Hacker*. New York, NY: Little, Brown and Company, 2011.

National Criminal Justice Reference Service. "Comprehensive Crime Control Act of 1984." National Criminal Justice Reference Service. Accessed May 5, 2014. www.ncjrs.gov/pdffiles1/Digitization/123365NCJRS.pdf.

Olson, Parmy. *We Are Anonymous: Inside The Hacker World of Lulzsec, Anonymous, and the Global Cyber Insurgency*. New York, NY: Little, Brown and Co., 2012.

Rapid7. "Vulnerability & Exploit Database | Rapid7." Vulnerability & Exploit Database. Accessed May 1, 2014. www.rapid7.com/db/modules.

RedSpin. "Penetration Testing Services & Security Audits: Proven Methodology. Exceptional Results." Redspin Penetration Testing, IT Security Assessments, HIPAA. Accessed May 10, 2014. www.redspin.com.

Richards, Tori. "Hacker Testifies News Corp Unit Hired Him." Reuters. Accessed April 26, 2014. www.reuters.com/article/2008/04/24/us-echostar-newscorp-idUSN2334980420080424?feedType=RSS&feedName=technologyNews&rpc=22&sp=true.

Shimomura, Tsutomu, and John Markoff. *Takedown: The Pursuit and Capture of Kevin Mitnick, America's Most Wanted Computer Outlaw—By the Man Who Did It*. New York, NY: Hyperion, 1996.

Simpson, Michael T., Kent Backman and James E. Corley. *Hands-on Ethical Hacking and Network Defense*. Boston, MA: Thomson Course Technology, 2013.

Tarnovsky, Christopher. Interview by Dr. Katherine Albrecht. Radio Broadcast. Appleton, WI, May 26, 2009.

"Top 10 Most Famous Hackers of All Time - IT Security." Accessed April 26, 2014. www.itsecurity.com/features/top-10-famous-hackers-042407.

U.S. Bureau of Labor Statistics. "Summary." U.S. Bureau of Labor Statistics. Accessed May 11, 2014. www.bls.gov/ooh/computer-and-information-technology/information-security-analysts.htm.

U.S. Department of Health & Human Services. "Who is Covered by the Privacy Rule." Health Information Privacy. Accessed May 29, 2014. www.hhs.gov/ocr/privacy/hipaa/understanding/summary/privacysummary.pdf.

Van Vleck, Tom. "How the Air Force Cracked Multics Security." Multics. Accessed May 5, 2014. www.multicians.org/security.html.

Venema, Wietse, and Dan Farmer. *Improving the Security of Your Site by Breaking into It*. www.csm.ornl.gov/~dunigan/cracking.html.

Wetzel, Joe. Interview by author. Personal interview. Appleton, WI, May 9, 2014.

# INDEX

Page numbers in **boldface** are illustrations.

White Hat Hacking

# ABOUT THE AUTHOR

JONATHAN SMITH is a server and mail systems engineer, currently working in the paper industry as a senior network planning analyst in Wisconsin. Security and security testing has been a part of his career for several years, particularly with website- and e-mail-related technologies such as spam control, intrusion detection, antivirus, and other defensive security measures. He enjoys hobbies such as ham radio, electronics, fishing, and spending time with his family. He hopes that this book will inspire young people to pursue a lifetime of learning, and to never stop asking "why" and "how."